# Personal Spiritual Warfare

# Protect Your TURF

## The "How To Do It" Book

### Also included:

### Bondage of the Threefold Cord

## A Teaching Manual

## by Thomas Velez

Thomas Velez

Dedicated to my loving wife Fay, who is the most dedicated, determined, and violent spiritual warrior for Jesus Christ that I know!

Unless otherwise indicated, Bible quotations are taken from the King James Version or New King James Version of the Bible.

References to Greek and Hebrew words and "Strong's" numbers are taken from The Exhaustive Concordance of the Bible, by James Strong

# Table of Contents

4

## INTRODUCTION

This Earth is becoming more and more divided and conflicted, between those that will follow God and those that will not. Many of those that will not follow God are strongly influenced by the personalities of the demonic realm, which are contrary to God and God's people. Such being the case, Christians are a natural target for the demonic realm, and the demons of that realm will resist the people of God: actively working against them and their families, their jobs, their businesses, their reputation, etc. Certainly, you have already experienced that. But know this, that "greater is He (Christ) that is in you, than he (the demonic, devils, etc.) that is in the world" (1 John 4:4). You have more power than your demonic enemies do. But, what is that power that you have and how do you use that power? How do you overcome those demonic forces, even influencing other people, in your everyday life? What are the current results in your life today?

The concepts and principles in this booklet of teaching spiritual warfare have been used since the late 1980s to teach people to actually DO spiritual warfare and WIN it. The demonic realm is in a war with God, and all those that align with God. If you are a Christian, then you are aligning yourself with God, and the demonic realm is at war with YOU! A war is made up of several battles over time. If you do not actively fight in a battle, you will not win in a battle.

This book is intended to place the "tools of spiritual war" into the hands of believers for them to use themselves. Why do spiritual warfare unless you fully intend to win it?

This booklet explains the concepts, gives scriptural backing for the concepts, and tells how to actually do it. Many actual examples are given. No prior experience or knowledge is necessary, only being a born-again Christian and having faith in Jesus Christ.

The best strategy of all, is to ask God what tool of prayer, declarations, commanding, or other action is the right one to use for any particular situation. It is good for us to know how to use all the tools of personal spiritual warfare, but it is always best to use God's strategy.

The biblical references are taken from the King James Bible or New King James Bible, and are clearly labeled, which allows for easy referencing to another version if desired. The Table of Contents is clear and detailed to allow easy lookup of the desired concepts for reference or review.

May God bless you, make you successful in spiritual warfare, and may He get the glory for the victories in your life.

# CHAPTER 1  Why Fight?

## A. Why Fight?

As Christians, we have chosen to align ourselves with Father God, the Creator of Heaven and Earth.  But, there is a war going on between God and Satan.  Since we have chosen to align ourselves with God, that automatically makes us enemy in the target of Satan and his forces.  Satan has a tendency to attack the weakest points of his enemies, you and me and our families.  We must defend ourselves and our families, and all that we are steward over: our "**TURF**".

Why is it that we, and our families, get so beaten down?  The answer lies beyond the physical realm, that which we can see and sense with our five natural human senses.  There is a war, with strategizing and plotting, being accomplished against us in the spirit realm, even working through other people (without them knowing it) against us.  Satan's attacks come against us, through cares of the world, relationships, finances, traumatic events, sicknesses, etc.  Why do so many of us get worn down after an extended fight against so many negative circumstances?

One reason is this.  We have all heard, of the Armor of God: Eph ch 6, but think about this.  If we depend upon our **shield of faith** only, for too long, that shield of faith gets beaten and pounded upon for so long and so many times, that that shield begins to lose its effectiveness in deflecting the attacks of the enemy, causing us to have more and more doubts and fears and anxiety and less and less faith, as time goes on, and that pounding against us continues. That wears us and our faith down over time.

THEN comes the pounding and beating upon our **breastplate** of righteousness-the last protection of our vitals: our character, our purity, our integrity. Satan brings temptations to try to defile us and make us feel vile and dirty and to despise ourselves.

Then the beating also comes upon our "**helmet** of salvation", getting us to question our self-worth or value, bringing guilt, depression, and a sense of hopelessness, and causing us to lose the willingness to fight and resist, even to the extreme of even losing the will to live.

*Prov 18:14 (Amp Ver) ¶ The strong spirit of a man sustains him in bodily pain or trouble, but a weak and broken spirit who can raise up or bear?*

Why does this happen?

Because, that person is **not using their sword enough** to keep the enemy far enough away from them: to keep the enemy from repeatedly beating and pounding upon their shield and breastplate.

That sword represents real spiritual warfare, using the specific word of God, and the name of Jesus Christ, declaring what God says, and also binding and commanding the demonic to leave: casting them out of and away from YOUR "**TURF**".

*Mt 11:12  And from the days of John the Baptist until now the kingdom of heaven suffereth violence, and the violent take it by force.*

- **We are in a war, and war is violent.**

*Rev 21:8 But the **cowardly**, unbelieving, abominable, murderers, sexually immoral, sorcerers, idolaters, and all liars shall have their part in the lake which burns with fire and brimstone, which is the second death.*

We have only one life to live.  Make the most of it.

**If you fight-you will win the war, one way or another, eventually.**

**If you do not fight-you will not win: you will not fulfil the destiny God has for you.**

**B. How Fit Are You?**

The Lord works with us:  Mark 16:20

*Mark 16:20 And they went forth, and preached every where, **the Lord working with them**, and confirming the word with signs following. Amen.*

Identify the enemy's strongholds and resistances in your life.

Ask yourself how fit am I for war? What do I need to improve?

- Mentally:
  - o What are your beliefs?
  - o What do you input to your mind? TV, reading, people, Internet, Bible
- Emotionally:
  - o existing emotions & even from your past; responses, feelings
- Spiritually:
  - o skill level in use of scriptures and gifts of the Holy Spirit.
- Physically:
  - o what inputs to your body: food, exercise
- Financially:
  - o existing & potential hindrances: robbery/losses, wastefulness
- Influence:
  - o your speech, knowledge, enthusiasm, success,

> caring/giving/ compassion for people

## C. What you feed yourself

Be careful what you feed yourself. Obviously, this includes what you eat physically to nourish your body, and supply energy for it, for proper growth, repair, and function. There's been much written about what food is good, and what is not good, for the human body and will I will not address that further here, except to say that that can place restrictions on one's physical body and obviously can cause limitations in traveling, etc.

But what is also just as important, is what we feed, our mind, will and emotions. What we feed it, is what we will become.

I once heard a story, an old story. I don't know where it originated, so I cannot give that person credit for the story, although I wish I could. As I remember, it goes like this

> There was once wise old Indian grandfather. He was talking to his grandson. He said to his grandson, "in every man's life, there is a war raging. There are two wolves fighting against each other, that whole man's life. One wolf is a good wolf: caring and loving and strong and defending the helpless and doing what is right. The other wolf is an

evil wolf, always trying to deceive, steal, hurt, kill and destroy, full of selfishness and greed and all evil things.

The little boy thought for a while in silence. Then he asked his grandfather "which wolf wins"?

The wise old grandfather said, "the one you feed."

## CHAPTER 2  The Birth & Preparation

### A.  Dominion
**God wanted and even intended for man to have dominion (power) over every living thing on the earth.**
No mention was made of the method to be used.

> *Genesis 1:26 And God said, Let us make man in our image, after our likeness: and let them* **have [dominion] over** *the fish of the sea, and over the fowl of the air, and over the cattle, and over all the earth, and over every creeping thing that creepeth upon the earth.*

> *Genesis 1:28 And God blessed them, and God said unto them, Be fruitful, and multiply, and replenish the earth, and subdue it: and* **have [dominion] over** *the fish of the sea, and over the fowl of the air, and over every living thing that moveth upon the earth.*

### B.  The Birth
**We are born in the Spirit when we are "Born Again".**
No supernatural Godly power lives in us until we are born into the Kingdom of God, because it is God that has authority over the forces of evil.

> *John 3:3 Jesus answered and said unto him, Verily, verily, I say unto thee, Except a man be born again, he cannot see the kingdom of God.*

*John 4:4 Nicodemus saith unto him, How can a man be born when he is old? can he enter the second time into his mother's womb, and be born?*

*John 3:5 Jesus answered, Verily, verily, I say unto thee, Except a man be born of water and {of} the **Spirit,** he cannot enter into the kingdom of God.*

*John 3:6 That which is born of the flesh is flesh; and that which is born of the Spirit is spirit.*

*John 3:7 Marvel not that I said unto thee, Ye must be born again.*

*John 3:16 For God so loved the world, that he gave his only begotten Son, that whosoever believeth in him should not perish, but have everlasting life.*

*John 3:17 For God sent not his Son into the world to condemn the world; but that the world through him might be saved.*

*John 3:18 He that believeth on him is not condemned: but he that believeth not is condemned already, because he hath not believed in the name of the only begotten Son of God.*

For more information on this, see the "Salvation" appendix at the end of this booklet.

**We are as babes in the spirit world.** Like any newborn, we begin our new spiritual life as babes, needing nutrition, sheltering, and loving protection. As newborns, we are not yet mature.

*1 Corinthians 3:1 And I, brethren, could not speak unto you as unto spiritual, but as unto* **carnal, {even} as unto babes in Christ.** *1 Corinthians 3:2 I have fed you with milk, and not with meat: for hitherto ye were not able {to bear it}, neither yet now are ye able. 1 Corinthians 3:3* **For ye are yet carnal:** *for whereas {there is} among you envying, and strife, and divisions, are ye not carnal, and walk as men?*

We need to be careful about what we feed the babes, or what the babes themselves put into themselves, if the babe is to survive, both in the natural and in the spiritual lives.

*Mt 5:8 Blessed are the pure in <u>heart</u>: for they shall see God.*

**We need the Baptism of the Holy Spirit with the evidence of speaking in tongues.** Many books have been written about this. Suffice it to say here that the power of God comes upon us after we have received this.

*Acts 1:8 But ye shall receive power, after that the Holy Ghost is come upon you: and ye shall be witnesses unto me both in Jerusalem, and in all Judaea, and in Samaria, and unto the uttermost part of the earth.*

Thomas Velez

## CHAPTER 3  The Growth: Understanding & Experience

**God wants us to grow spiritually by learning. Learning comes by understanding.**

**Understanding comes by the WORD OF GOD through reading, studying, hearing, and teachings.**

> *Romans 10:17 So then faith {cometh} by hearing, and **hearing by the word of God.***

> *1 Peter 2:2 As newborn [babes], desire the sincere **milk of the word,** that ye may grow thereby:*

**Understanding also comes by doing, or EXPERIENCE.**
Someone once said something like; the man with an experience is never at the mercy of the man with a theory.  Experience becomes both a teacher to us and an indelible mark upon us.  To some extent, we also learn by trial and error.  If we don't try, how do we personally know that it works?  How can we give a testimony if we did not experience something?

> *Hebrews 5:12 For when for the time ye ought to be teachers, ye have need that one teach you again which {be} the first principles of*

*the oracles of God; and are become such as have need of milk, and not of strong meat.*
*Hebrews 5:13 For every one that useth milk {is} unskilful in the word of righteousness: for he is a babe.*
*Hebrews 5:14 But strong meat belongeth to them that are of full age, {even} those who* **by reason of use have their senses exercised** *to discern both good and evil.*

*Colossians 1:10 That ye might walk worthy of the Lord unto all pleasing, being fruitful in every good work, and increasing in the knowledge of God;*

Of course, some things are best not tried, especially when there can be permanent damage to us, such as putting our hand in a fire, or jumping off a high cliff.

The getting started on this road of experience and growth, the Lord God makes our salvation and our initial relationship with Him exciting. Upon accepting Jesus Christ as our Lord and Savior, we begin our walk with him. That initial walk is very exciting, and we may see many wondrous things done by Him for us in our lives, all depending upon our expectations of Him. Those wondrous things that he does, in us and for us, cause us to be excited and want to learn more about Him and become closer to Him, and even to tell others about what has happened to us.

Jesus watches how we respond after our initial salvation experience with Him. He has given us a taste of Himself and His goodness and love for us.  He expects us to respond to that.  He expects us to come after Him and seek Him.

Normally, after an initial period, it seems that the Lord slowly withdraws His presence from us, and we don't sense Him the way we did initially, and He doesn't seem to be as involved in our lives as He was.  This is because the Lord wants us to actively seek Him.  He wants us to do that by reading His word, the Bible, by praying and talking to Him, spending time with Him and meditating about Him, and seeking to find out what He wants us to do, and to change, and to quit.

This is where many people seem to fall away from the Lord.  They expect this initial excitement, like a lust, for God to continue, but it doesn't seem to.  They get disillusioned, and think that God has left them, or that God doesn't care anymore, or is just irrelevant to them in their lives.  In the Bible, Mark chapter 4 warns us of this falling away from that closeness to God.

*Mark 4:14 The sower soweth the word.*
*15 And these are they by the way side, where the word is sown; but when they have heard, Satan cometh immediately, and taketh away the word that was sown in their hearts.*
*16 And these are they likewise which are sown on stony ground; who, when they*

*have heard the word, immediately receive
it with gladness;
17 And have no root in themselves, and so
endure but for a time: afterward, when
affliction or persecution ariseth for the
word's sake, immediately they are
offended.*

After God has given us a taste of Himself, and
has begun to seemingly withdraw Himself from
us, to get us to follow Him to seek after Him, we
will begin to experience many things. Many of
these things will seem hard to us. There are two
reasons for this.

First, we have chosen to take sides with God and
Jesus in a war that encompasses our known
environment, namely war between God and
Satan. That war naturally includes the followers
of each. Since we are now followers of God, we
are the enemies of Satan, and Satan will try to
attack and harm us in any way he can.

Second, God will use the experiences in our life,
good and bad, to teach us and help us to grow and
learn to depend upon Him, and learn to use the
gifting's and the gifts that He has given us, both,
natural gifts and spiritual gifts, in the natural
realm and in the spiritual realm.

We live in a fallen world, and many bad things,
will befall us, and those we love. This is also the
fate of all human beings, for all of history. There

are diseases, wars, catastrophes, etc., and such as is common to all mankind. We can learn to lean on Jesus to help us make it through these things, and to seek God in the midst of these things, even for divine intervention. At times. But, sometimes we just have to go through those things. It is not God that comes to steal, kill, and destroy, that is Satan's job description.

> *John 10:10 The thief (Satan/devils) cometh not, but for to steal, and to kill, and to destroy: I am come that they might have life, and that they might have it more abundantly.*

Sometimes, this is where people fall out of love with God, even blaming God for the catastrophes in their lives, to the point of being angry with God, or even hating Him, when God had nothing to do with it. God does not want to hurt us.

God wants to make us stronger, and to grow and be strong, and wise, and be able to fulfill His great plans for us: for us to fulfill our destiny.

To do this, we will have to go through many life experiences, and also go through His specific training to prepare us for our destiny. This is just like we would expect in the natural or physical world. Just like a physical baby in our world would have to go through things such as diaper training, and experience hurts and falls, bullying, disappointments, being told no, etc., etc., we also go through such things in the spiritual world. Our spiritual being has to go through training as we, a spiritual child, grow up, such as school, learning skills, wisdom, and maturity.

Through this process, the child is to learn discipline, by being disciplined by the parents, hopefully for the child's good. A good parent disciplines the child to teach them what is good, and right, and safe. God does the same thing for His children. Sometimes, in the natural children become rebellious, and choose to do things their own way, sometimes bringing upon themselves much harm, which might not have happened if they had obeyed their parents. Likewise, it is the same in the spirit realm. Many times people choose and do things which bring them much harm, as a result of what they themselves chose to do. Naturally, God did not want us to be rebellious, but similarly He wants us to learn and grow and to do that which is good and right and safe, with respect to our spiritual lives.

As we grow older, both in the natural and in the spiritual realm, we are supposed to have learned to replace parental discipline, self-discipline, inherently knowing. In most cases, what is good and right and safe. We would not think it normal for a child of 18 years old not to know how to tie their shoelaces, and to be constantly asking for someone else to do it for them. Why then, do we think it normal for a person having been a Christian for 18 years, to constantly ask others to interpret the Bible for them, or to make good and right and safe decisions about spiritual things. What have these people been doing for those 18 years? Have they been reading their Bible, and studying, and seeking God for those 18 years?

God expects people to grow, and their spiritual maturity, as time goes on. If they are seeking God, He will mentor them personally, or provide learning experiences in a safe environment for them. One such area is this, is in personal spiritual warfare. God wants us to be strong warriors in his Army. As such, he will provide training for us, such as boot camp for the military general forces, and specialized training for each of us in the arena that he would have us go into: to prepare us for our individual destiny.

In the boot camp for personal spiritual warfare, God will provide safe, though possibly frightening, experiences in battling the demonic realm which comes against us. God will provide these experiences so that we learn to use the gifts and tools that He gives to us to learn to overcome these demonic enemies. When we learn these things, we can then teach them to others. Hopefully, that those others will listen, they may not have to learn the lessons the hard way, but learn from the experiences and successes of others. In His boot camp, there may be live spiritual ammunition being fired, to and from the enemy, but the end result will be that you are not permanently harmed, and you will have learned how to prevent and/or repel such attacks in the

future, and be able to tell others how you did it.
You may actually have encounters with real
demons, fully sensing them, and perhaps even
seeing them. You may feel them attacking your
body somehow, but remember:

> *1Jo 4:4 Ye are of God, little children, and
> have overcome them: because greater is
> He that is in you, than he that is in the
> world.*

> *Luke 10:19 Behold, I give unto you power
> to tread on serpents and scorpions, and
> over all the power of the enemy: and
> nothing shall by any means hurt you.*

**The name of JESUS overpowers everything!
Speak it whenever you need to!**

We live in a real world, but the most real-world
of all, is the spiritual world or realm. The
spiritual world influences what goes on in the real
world far beyond what we could even think or
imagine, both for good and for bad. That is why
spiritual battles, and prayer warriors, often keep
physical battles and physical catastrophes and
demonic strategies and control from being
successful against God's children. There is much
less bloodshed when the battle is in the spiritual
world and prevented from coming into the
physical world. Thus, it behooves us to defend
ourselves, and our "**turf**", and that which is
around us and exercises authority over us. (Our
"**turf**" is ourselves, our family, and all that we are

steward over, such as our home, our vehicles, our job, etc.)

In the chapters to come, I will be explaining various tools that can be used in accomplishing personal spiritual warfare, to protect yourself and your turf.

Thomas Velez

## CHAPTER 4  The Power

### A.  Jesus has the power, and gave us the power.  The power is in us.

It was Jesus' intent to give us the power, and it was His desire that we actually use what He gave us.  It is not just knowing something, but Jesus' commands that we DO something.

We should learn to obey God, both through the written word of God, the Bible.  God does not change.  The things that God says, and the concepts that He has written in the Bible, such as marriage, being between a man and a woman, has not changed, and will not change.  God also wants us to follow the conscience that He has given us, and not for us to resist that conscience so long as to sear it over, so that it no longer nudges us to do that which is right and pleasing to God.

> *James 4:7 Submit yourselves therefore to God.  Resist the [devil], and he will flee from you.*

Power comes into us, after we receive the fullness of the Holy Spirit, or Holy Ghost, with the evidence of speaking in tongues.

> *Acts 1:8 But **ye shall receive power, after that the Holy Ghost is come upon you:** and ye shall be witnesses unto me both in Jerusalem,*

*and in all Judaea, and in Samaria, and unto
the uttermost part of the earth.
Acts 1:9 And when he had spoken these
things, while they beheld, he was taken up;
and a cloud received him out of their sight.*

*Ac 2:4 And they were all filled with the Holy
Ghost, and began to speak with other tongues,
as the Spirit gave them utterance.*

Not everyone or every spirit that claims to follow
God or Jesus is really from God.
*1 John 4:3 And every spirit that confesseth
not that Jesus Christ is come in the flesh is
not of God: and this is that {spirit} of
antichrist, whereof ye have heard that it
should come; and even now already is it in
the world.*

But the Holy Spirit in us is more powerful than
any other:

*1 John 4:4 Ye are of God, little children, and
have overcome them: because greater is he
that is in you, than he that is in the world.*

After the resurrection of Jesus, all power was
given to Jesus, and Jesus will be with us:

*Matthew 28:16 Then the eleven disciples went
away into Galilee, into a mountain where
Jesus had appointed them.
Matthew 28:17 And when they saw him, they*

*worshipped him: but some doubted.*
*Matthew 28:18 And Jesus came and spake*
*unto them, saying, All power is given unto me*
*in heaven and in earth.*
*Matthew 28:19 Go ye therefore, and teach all*
*nations, baptizing them in the name of the*
*Father, and of the Son, and of the Holy*
*Ghost:*
*Matthew 28:20 Teaching them to observe all*
*things whatsoever I have commanded you:*
*and, lo, I am with you alway, {even} unto the*
*end of the world. Amen.*

And Jesus give this power to those that follow
and obey Him (becoming His disciples).

*Luke 10:17 And the seventy returned again*
*with joy, saying, Lord, even the devils are*
*subject unto us through thy name.*
*Luke 10:18 And he said unto them, I beheld*
*Satan as lightning fall from heaven.*
*Luke 10:19 Behold, I give unto you power to*
*tread on serpents and scorpions, and over all*
*the power of the enemy: and nothing shall by*
*any means hurt you.*
*Luke 10:20 Notwithstanding in this rejoice*
*not, that the spirits are subject unto you; but*
*rather rejoice, because your names are*
*written in heaven.*

We each have power through Christ, because of
His love for us, but that power is according to
how we work it.  Will we learn to use it, or will

we choose not to?  Do not hold back because of fear, as so many, if not most people, do.

> *Ephesians 3:19 And to know the love of Christ, which passeth knowledge, that ye might be filled with all the fulness of God. Ephesians 3:20 Now unto him that is able to do exceeding abundantly above all that we ask or think, according to the power that worketh in us,*

We need to think and discern and strategize and war spiritually.  Even though it may be much like the natural world, we must realize it is happening in a reality where most do not see or sense, and therefore do not even know it is happening, and thus do not defend against it or resist it at all.

*2 Corinthians 10:3 For though we walk in the flesh, we do not war after the flesh:*
*2 Corinthians 10:4 (For the weapons of our warfare {are} not carnal, but mighty through God to the pulling down of strong holds;)*
*2 Corinthians 10:5 Casting down imaginations, and every high thing that exalteth itself against the knowledge of God, and bringing into captivity every thought to the obedience of Christ;*
*2 Corinthians 10:6 And having in a readiness to revenge all disobedience, when your obedience is fulfilled.*

## B.  There is power for healing, signs & wonders in the name of Jesus:

Jesus gave us this power to use in our everyday life, and to help others as well as ourselves.

> *Mark 16:17 And these signs shall follow them that believe;* **In my name shall they cast out devils;** *they shall speak with new tongues; Mark 16:18 They shall take up serpents; and if they drink any deadly thing, it shall not hurt them; they shall lay hands on the sick, and they shall recover.*

> *Acts 4:30 By stretching forth thine hand* **to heal; and that signs and wonders may be done by the [name] of thy holy child Jesus.**

## C.  There is power in the blood of Jesus, to forgive sins.

> *1 John 1:7 But if we walk in the light, as he is in the light, we have fellowship one with another, and the [blood] of Jesus Christ his Son cleanseth us from all sin.*

> *Hebrews 9:14 How much more shall the blood of Christ, who through the eternal Spirit offered himself without spot to God, purge your conscience from dead works to serve the living God?*

**D. There is power in the blood of Jesus to destroy the works of the devil:**

*Hebrews 2:14 Forasmuch then as the children are partakers of flesh and [blood], he also himself likewise took part of the same; that through death he might destroy him that had the power of death, that is, the devil;*

**E. The Blood of Jesus seals God's Covenant with us, & enables us to live a life pleasing to God:**

*Hebrews 13:20 Now the God of peace, that brought again from the dead our Lord Jesus, that great shepherd of the sheep, through the blood of the everlasting covenant, Hebrews 13:21 **Make you perfect in every good work to do his will, working in you that which is well pleasing in his sight,** through Jesus Christ; to whom {be} glory for ever and ever. Amen.*

## CHAPTER 5  The Attitude

God desires us to have an attitude of being humble and submitted to Him, but to be active, bold and FORCEFULLY resist/fight against the devil (the kingdom and forces of darkness).

> *James 4:6 "God resists the proud, But gives grace to the humble"*
> *7 Therefore* **submit to God. Resist the devil and he will flee from you.**
> *8 Draw near to God and He will draw near to you.*

> *James 3:16 For* **where envy and self-seeking exist, confusion and every evil thing are there.**

God wants us to be very bold and very courageous.  He wants us to be fearless, and to represent Him that way, especially in the face of people's opposition to Him.  If you want to represent God, you must represent Him this way in the face of opposition to Him!

> *Joshua 1:7 Only* **be thou strong and very courageous,** *that thou mayest observe to do according to all the law, which Moses my servant commanded thee: turn not from it {to} the right hand or {to} the left, that thou mayest prosper whithersoever thou goest.*
> *Joshua 1:8* **This book of the law shall not**

*depart out of thy mouth; but thou shalt meditate therein day and night, that thou mayest observe to do according to all that is written therein: for then thou shalt make thy way prosperous, and then thou shalt have good success.*

*Joshua 1:9* **Have not I commanded thee? Be strong and of a good courage; be not afraid, neither be thou dismayed:** *for the LORD thy God {is} with thee whithersoever thou goest.*

*Joshua 1:10 Then Joshua commanded the officers of the people, saying,*

*Joshua 1:11 Pass through the host, and command the people, saying, Prepare you victuals; for within three days ye shall pass over this Jordan, to* **go in to possess** *the land, which the LORD your God giveth you to possess it.*

We must think of this as a war, and be willing to even be violent. We must also be willing to endure hardness, like any soldier in the natural world.

*Mt 11:12 And from the days of John the Baptist until now the kingdom of heaven* <u>suffereth</u> <u>violence</u>*, and the violent take it by force.*

*2 Timothy 2:3 Thou therefore* **endure hardness,** *as a good soldier of Jesus Christ.*
*2 Timothy 2:4* **No man that warreth entangleth himself with the affairs of {this}**

*life; that he may please him who hath chosen him to be a soldier.*

We cannot just sit back and relax and ignore the spiritual attacks and devices against us. The enemy will use the unrestricted time we give him to build a cage to contain and control us. The enemy will use finances, family members, sicknesses, other people, our jobs, and even our government to bring us down and try to overcome us, even to get us to just give up trying. The devil's desire is to control us, ensnare and capture us and make us ineffective: to overcome us. We must **be alert and NEVER QUIT.**

*1 Peter 5:8* ***[Be sober], [be vigilant];*** *because your adversary the devil, as a roaring lion, walketh about, seeking whom he may devour:*

Thomas Velez

## CHAPTER 6  Verbal Actions

### A.  Praying: Asking God to do it for us:

This is what we first learn to do as new Christians.  We can pray aloud or silently.  God and Jesus hear us either way. **When we pray, we are asking God** to do something for us.

> *2 Kings 6:18 And when they came down to him, Elisha **prayed** unto the LORD, and said, Smite this people, I pray thee, with blindness. And he smote them with blindness according to the word of Elisha.*

Now, in the New Testament, we can **ask in the name of Jesus**.

> *John 14:13 And whatsoever ye shall **ask in My name**, that will I do, that the Father may be glorified in the Son.*
> *John 14:14 If ye shall ask any thing in My name, I will do it.*
>
> *John 16:23 And in that day ye shall ask Me nothing. Verily, verily, I say unto you, Whatsoever ye shall ask the Father in My name, he will give it you.*

### B.  Unity: Agreement in prayer:

When two or more are praying together.  We generally pray this kind of prayer aloud, by at least one person, because to come into agreement, one person needs to express what it is that they are coming into agreement about.

*Matthew 18:19 Again I say unto you, That if two of you shall **agree** on earth as touching any thing that they shall ask, it shall be done for them of my Father which is in heaven. Matthew 18:20 For where two or three are gathered together in my name, there am I in the midst of them.*

## C. Praising & Singing:

God does warfare on our behalf when we praise and sing to Him. Since He inhabits us and also inhabits our praises, our enemies become His enemies and He helps us. We can praise Him silently or aloud, but singing is generally done aloud.

*Psalms 9:1 To the chief Musician upon Muthlabben, A Psalm of David. I will praise {thee}, O LORD, with my whole heart; I will show forth all thy marvellous works. Psalms 9:2 I will be glad and rejoice in thee: I will sing praise to thy name, O thou most High. Psalms 9:3 When mine enemies are turned back, they shall fall and perish at thy presence. Psalms 9:4 For thou hast maintained my right and my cause; thou satest in the throne judging right. Psalms 9:5 Thou hast rebuked the heathen, thou hast destroyed the wicked, thou hast put out their name for ever and ever.*

*Ps 22:3 But thou art holy, O thou that* **inhabitest the praises** *of Israel.*

*2 Chronicles 20:14 Then upon Jahaziel the son of Zechariah, the son of Benaiah, the son of Jeiel, the son of Mattaniah, a Levite of the sons of Asaph, came the Spirit of the LORD in the midst of the congregation;*
*2 Chronicles 20:15 And he said, Hearken ye, all Judah, and ye inhabitants of Jerusalem, and thou king Jehoshaphat, Thus saith the LORD unto you,* **Be not afraid nor dismayed by reason of this great multitude; for the battle {is} not yours, but God's.**
*2 Chronicles 20:16 To morrow go ye down against them: behold, they come up by the cliff of Ziz; and ye shall find them at the end of the brook, before the wilderness of Jeruel.*
*2 Chronicles 20:17 Ye shall not {need} to fight in this {battle}: set yourselves, stand ye {still}, and see the salvation of the LORD with you, O Judah and Jerusalem:* **fear not, nor be dismayed**; *tomorrow go out against them: for the LORD {will be} with you.*
*2 Chronicles 20:18 And Jehoshaphat bowed his head with {his} face to the ground: and all Judah and the inhabitants of Jerusalem fell before the LORD, worshipping the LORD.*
*2 Chronicles 20:19 And the Levites, of the children of the Kohathites, and of the children of the Korhites, stood up to praise the LORD*

*God of Israel with a loud voice on high.*
*2 Chronicles 20:20 And they rose early in the morning, and went forth into the wilderness of Tekoa: and as they went forth, Jehoshaphat stood and said, Hear me, O Judah, and ye inhabitants of Jerusalem; Believe in the LORD your God, so shall ye be established; believe his prophets, so shall ye prosper.*
*2 Chronicles 20:21 And when he had consulted with the people, he appointed* <u>*singers*</u> *unto the LORD, and that should praise the beauty of holiness, as they went out before the army, and to say, Praise the LORD; for his mercy {endureth} for ever.*
*2 Chronicles 20:22 And* **when they began to sing and to praise, the LORD set ambushments against** *the children of Ammon, Moab, and mount Seir, which were come against Judah; and they were smitten.*
*2 Chronicles 20:23 For the children of Ammon and Moab stood up against the inhabitants of mount Seir, utterly to slay and destroy {them}: and when they had made an end of the inhabitants of Seir, every one helped to destroy another.*
*2 Chronicles 20:24 And when Judah came toward the watch tower in the wilderness, they looked unto the multitude, and, behold, they {were} dead bodies fallen to the earth, and none escaped.*

## D.  Hearing God's-Specific Battle Plan/Knowing the enemy's plan

God can also give us specific battle plans, such as was given in 2 Chronicles chapter 20 above. Also reference the story of Gideon in Judges chapter 7, Joshua at the Battle of Jericho in Judges chapter 6 and Elisha in 2 Kings chapter 6. We simply pray for God to show us.

> *2 Kings 6:12 And one of his servants said, None, my lord, O king (of Syria) but Elisha, the prophet that {is} in Israel, telleth the king of Israel the words that thou speakest in thy bedchamber.*

This shows us that God can reveal the plans of the enemy, to us, of both demonic enemies and physical enemies.

## E.  Declaring: Claiming/Proclaiming Scriptures

When we read the Bible, we can claim the promise of God that we see there that are for us. When we need a prayer answered, we can pray in accordance with what God has already said in His word.  To make this most effective, we can proclaim or **DECLARE** this word of God, **aloud, even loudly**, proclaiming it to both the spiritual world and the natural world.  The spoken word of God has power, even creative power.  Even the world was created by the spoken word of God (John chapter one).

Jesus even quoted and proclaimed scriptures to the devil.

**There is also no record in the Bible of Jesus commanding any devils silently.**

God hears our silent prayers, the devil does not. We never ask or pray to the devil(s) about anything!  As will be shown later, the devil has to obey you when you properly speak the word of God, in Jesus name. Since **the devil also does not hear any of your silent commands**, he is not responsible to God to obey your silent commands or proclamations-they must be spoken aloud for the devil to hear and obey.  We cannot resist the devil silently.

> *Matthew 4:10 Then saith Jesus unto him, Get thee hence, Satan: for **it is written**, Thou shalt worship the Lord thy God, and him only shalt thou serve.*
> *Matthew 4:11 Then the devil leaveth him, and, behold, angels came and ministered unto him.*

A great proclamation or declaration of scriptures for us to declare loudly is:
> *Psalms 91:1 He that dwelleth in the secret place of the most High shall abide under the shadow of the Almighty.*
> *Psalms 91:2 I will say of the LORD, {He is} my refuge and my fortress: my God; in him will I trust.*

*Psalms 91:3 Surely he shall deliver thee from the snare of the fowler, {and} from the noisome pestilence.*
*Psalms 91:4 He shall cover thee with his feathers, and under his wings shalt thou trust: his truth {shall be thy} shield and buckler."*
*Psalms 91:5 Thou shalt not be afraid for the terror by night; {nor} for the arrow {that} flieth by day;*
*Psalms 91:6 {Nor} for the pestilence {that} walketh in darkness; {nor} for the destruction {that} wasteth at noonday.*
*Psalms 91:7 A thousand shall fall at thy side, and ten thousand at thy right hand; {but} it shall not come nigh thee.*
*Psalms 91:8 Only with thine eyes shalt thou behold and see the reward of the wicked.*
*Psalms 91:9 Because thou hast made the LORD, {which is} my refuge, {even} the most High, thy habitation;*
*Psalms 91:10 There shall no evil befall thee, neither shall any plague come nigh thy dwelling.*
*Psalms 91:11 For he shall give his angels charge over thee, to keep thee in all thy ways.*
*Psalms 91:12 They shall bear thee up in {their} hands, lest thou dash thy foot against a stone.*
*Psalms 91:13 Thou shalt tread upon the lion and adder: the young lion and the dragon shalt thou trample under feet.*
*Psalms 91:14 Because he hath set his love upon me, therefore will I deliver him: I will*

*set him on high, because he hath known my name.*
*Psalms 91:15 He shall call upon me, and I will answer him: I {will be} with him in trouble; I will deliver him, and honour him.*
*Psalms 91:16 With long life will I satisfy him, and show him my salvation.*

**It is if we are declaring/proclaiming the law/decrees of God the Almighty unto both spiritual world and the physical world, which must be obeyed!**

**F. Binding the enemy (strong man):**
As was shown above, we must do this aloud, not silently, since the devil cannot hear us to obey unless we speak up.

*Mark 3:27 No man can enter into a strong man's house, and spoil his goods, except he will **first [bind]** the strong man; and then he will spoil his house.*

An example of this is: **"in the name of Jesus Christ, I bind you devil of lust. I bind your hands, your feet, your mouth, and command you not to cause any commotion"**. We bind the devil/strongman before we cast him out. This is to prohibit him from fighting back or resisting us or causing a commotion or manifestation. We use the name of Jesus because it has authority over all devils.

*Philippians 2:10 That at the name of Jesus every knee should bow, of {things} in heaven, and {things} in earth, and {things} under the earth;*

## G. Casting out devils in the name of Jesus:
We should only cast out demons from **Christians**. Why?

1. The demons can and will return to that non-Christian person, because they do not have the Spirit of God within them (their house meaning their body) is empty.
2. Also, they will be worse off than before, because the demon(s) cast out will return with more and stronger demons.

*Mt 12:45 Then goeth he, and taketh with himself seven other spirits more wicked than himself, and they enter in and dwell there: and the last state of that man is worse than the first.*

We should only cast out demons from **willing** Christians. Why?

1. God gives all people a free will. A person can choose to keep a demon and continue to partake of what he/she and the demon wants. It is not God's will to overrule a person's free will. Therefore, we also should not use God's power to do anything against God's will,

if even we could.

2. One of at least three possibilities of resistance by the demonic. To be effective, each of the follow, paragraphs a-c, must be addressed and corrected.

    a. The demons are legalists. They may claim a right to remain because of whatever loopholes exist in the law of the universe- God's law. Sometimes, the person does not want to give up their sin or demon. This person must want to give up their sin/demon and repent and fully intend to change their behavior to be pleasing to God.

    b. The demons are legalists. They may claim legal right to be in/or harass a person because of prior contracts/dedications by that person's parent or ancestor. All previous contracts with or dedications to the demonic in all forms, must be renounced and repented for. This is done by the person who is being cleansed (not by the person who did the contract or dedication. They may be long since dead). The person being cleansed is formally and verbally "breaking the contract/covenant" with the demonic. Then the blood and power of Jesus Christ can and will set them free!

c. The demons are legalists. They may claim the right to resist because of the sin of the person's ancestors, and the penalty/curse is carried down to the 3rd or 4th generation of those people that hate God. This is called a **"generational curse".** Stopping the curse is done by the cleansing blood of Jesus. This again is done by the person renouncing the sins and curses of their ancestor(s). These generational curses in either or both the spiritual or the physical realm.

*Ex 20:5 Thou shalt not bow down thyself to them, nor serve them: for I the LORD thy God am a jealous God, visiting the iniquity of the fathers upon the children unto the third and fourth generation of them that hate me.*

Examples of things that **MIGHT** be a generational curse;
- Habits, sins, sicknesses, or illness of your ancestors, such as:
    - cancer, diabetes, alcoholism, depression, anger, poverty, adultery, lust, divorce, gossip, unbelief, greed, gluttony

The root cause may have been their involvement in the Masonic Lodges, or Witchcraft, Occult, etc.

*2 Cor 5:17 Therefore if any man be in Christ, he is a new creature: old things are passed away; behold, all things are become new.*

3. Since the demon(s) cast out will quickly return, it gives people the impression that casting out the demon(s) did not work. When the actuality of it was that they quickly left because they had to, and then they quickly returned because they could, sometimes almost immediately.

We do this aloud. Remember:

**There is also no record in the Bible of Jesus commanding any devils silently.**

*Matthew 10:1 And when he had called unto {him} his twelve disciples, he gave them [power] {against} unclean spirits, to cast them out, and to heal all manner of sickness and all manner of disease.*

*Mark 9:38 And John answered him, saying, Master, we saw one casting out devils **in thy [name]**, and he followeth not us: and we forbad him, because he followeth not us. Mark 9:39 But Jesus said, Forbid him not: for there is no man which shall do a miracle **in my [name]**, that can lightly speak evil of me.*

*Mark 16:17 And these signs shall follow them that believe; **In my [name]** shall they cast out devils; they shall speak with new tongues;*

*Luke 10:17 And the seventy returned again with joy, saying, Lord, even the devils are subject unto us **through thy [name].***

*Ephesians 1:20 Which he wrought in Christ, when he raised him from the dead, and set {him} at his own right hand in the heavenly {places},*
*Ephesians 1:21 Far above all principality, and power, and might, and dominion, and every name that is named, not only in this world, but also in that which is to come:*
*Ephesians 1:22 And hath put all {things} under his feet, and gave him {to be} the head over all {things} to the church,*

*Philippians 2:9 Wherefore God also hath
highly exalted him, and given Him a name
which is above every name:*

*Philippians 2:10 That **at the name of Jesus**
every knee should bow, of {things} in heaven,
and {things} in earth, and {things} under the
earth;*

We cast out devils forcefully.   Normally, when
we have confidence through experience, we just
speak in a normal voice tone/level and tell the
demon of (name a function or personality trait of
the demon, such as: anger, insecurity, fear, lust,
addiction, revenge, etc.).  The demons recognize
the authority and presence of Christ within us.
They also recognize the physical appearance of
human frailty and insecurity-by our
human/physical manners, expressions, speech,
etc.  Remember, the demonic has been around
human beings for many thousands of years, so
they have learned our typical reactions, body
language, etc.-all being external INDICATIONS
of our real faith: do we really believe that we can
and will cast out the demon?

We use verbal forcefulness when necessary, but
we always use firmness.  We first bind the devils
as explained above.  We usually cast out the main
devils one by one in the name of Jesus: by
commanding them to leave, in the name, the
power, the authority, and the blood of Jesus

Christ.

> **In the name of Jesus Christ, I/we command you demons of _____ to leave, in the name, the power, the authority, and the blood of Jesus Christ.**

After the principal devils in a person's life (their strongholds) are cast out, then we can easily go after the remainder that can be identified.

In casting out the devils that harass us or a person we are ministering to (with their permission), we need not fear the devil, because the Bible says that:

> *1 John 4: 4 Ye are of God, little children, and have overcome them: because **greater is He that is in you, than he that is in the world.***

> *Luke 10:19 Behold, I **give unto you power** to tread on serpents and scorpions, and over all the power of the enemy: and **nothing shall by any means hurt you.***

## H.  COMMANDING: Speaking to the problem/enemy

Here we are speaking directly to (or commanding) to something; whether it be an obstacle, a devil, or a natural phenomenon (such as a storm coming our way).  We are **COMMANDING it** to remove itself, in the name of Jesus.

Paul commanded (aloud) a devil to leave a
person:

> *Acts 16:18 And this did she many days. But
> Paul, being grieved, turned and **said to the
> spirit, I command thee in the [name] of
> Jesus Christ** to come out of her. And he came
> out the same hour.*

Jesus explained that we could command an
obstacle (i.e. a circumstance);

> *Matthew 17:20 And Jesus said unto them,
> Because of your unbelief: for verily I say unto
> you, If ye have faith as a grain of mustard
> seed, **ye shall say unto this [mountain],**
> Remove hence to yonder place; **and it shall**
> remove; and nothing shall be impossible unto
> you.*

Jesus commanded a storm to be still:

> *Mark 4:39 And He arose, and rebuked the
> wind, and **said unto the sea**, Peace, be still.
> And the wind ceased, and there was a great
> calm.*

I have commanded storms coming my way to
dissipate harmlessly for almost 40 years and have
always seen successful results.  Not once did this
ever fail.  I have seen tornados, high winds, heavy
rain, and even flooding stop before reaching
myself, my family, or my home: **MY TURF**.  As

an example, stand up, face the storm and with authority loudly say something like "**in the name of Jesus, I command** any storm approaching myself, my family, my home, my vehicles, my Church, or my place of work to **go back up into the atmosphere and dissipate harmlessly**".  At other times I have commanded "in the name of Jesus Christ, **I command this flooding to stop before it reaches my home**".  This **ALWAYS** works.

## I. Prophesying

We can wage warfare with the prophecies that God has given us, either directly or through someone else.  As we speak this loudly, we are proclaiming God's word with power.  We proclaim or declare this word of God to both the spiritual world and the natural word.  The spoken word of God has power, **even creative power**. Even the world was created by the spoken word of God (John chapter one).

> *1 Timothy 1:18 This charge I commit unto thee, son Timothy, according to the prophecies which went before on thee, that thou **by them** mightest war a good warfare; 1 Timothy 1:19 Holding faith, and a good conscience; which some having put away concerning faith have made shipwreck:*

We can actually read the prophesy loudly, such as "God has said ......(prophesy)............. , so in the name of Jesus Christ I command the spiritual world and the natural world to line up with and obey God's word"!

### J. Commission Angels

Here, we ask God to give or commission His angels to work on our behalf. Many angels are already doing this, but sometimes we have specific requests for them to do.

> *Hebrews 1:14 Are they not all ministering spirits, sent forth **to minister for them** who shall be heirs of salvation?*

> *Psalms 91:11 For he shall give his angels charge over thee, to keep thee in all thy ways. Psalms 91:12 They shall bear thee up in {their} hands, lest thou dash thy foot against a stone.*

In doing this, we first want to **ask God for a strategy, then assign angels a task or mission to fulfill, subject to the approval of God**, who is the only one who can really command His angels.

As an example: "In the name of Jesus Christ, I/we commission angels in accordance with Hebrews 1:14, and with the approval of God, to
...............................

Usually, I quote Hebrews1:14 also:

*Heb 1:14 Are they not all ministering spirits, sent forth to minister for them who shall be heirs of salvation?*

Examples of missions for angels might be:

- In the name of Jesus Christ, I/we commission angels, with the approval of God, to go and retrieve a certain child from the clutches of _____(the enemy: perhaps a gang, a drug place, place of prostitution or slavery, etc.) and bring them back home.  I have seen this work several times.
- In the name of Jesus Christ, I/we commission angels, with the approval of God, to go and retrieve a certain lost object and bring it back.  I have also seen this work several times.

I have seen in visions (which many times are symbolic of what we might understand in our own world/experience) where what actually happens is that the angels first listen to us, and then "look back" to God for His approval, and then God nods His head, indicating His approval for them to do that.  God really does not need to "nod His head" to give His approval, but it is symbolically showing me/us that He approves the mission/task assignment.

## K.  Shout:
Shouting seems to pierce the air, splitting the power of the prince of the air-the devil.

*Ephesians 2:2 Wherein in time past ye walked according to the course of this world, according to the **prince of the power of the air**, the spirit that now worketh in the children of disobedience:*

Judges 7:20 *And the three companies blew the trumpets, and brake the pitchers, and held the lamps in their left hands, and the trumpets in their right hands to blow {withal}: and they **cried**, The sword of the LORD, and of [Gideon].*

Joshua 6:16 *And it came to pass at the seventh time, when the priests blew with the trumpets, Joshua said unto the people, **Shout;** for the LORD hath given you the city.*

Matthew 11:12 *And from the days of John the Baptist until now the kingdom of heaven [suffereth violence], and **the violent take it by force.***

Psalms 47:1 *To the chief Musician, A Psalm for the sons of Korah. O [clap] your hands, all ye people; **shout** unto God with the voice of triumph.*
Psalms 47:2 *For the LORD most high {is} terrible; {he is} a great King over all the earth.*
Psalms 47:3 *He shall subdue the people under us, and the nations under our feet.*

We do this by shouting loudly, claiming what we want, God's promises, God's words, or praising God/Jesus or thanking Him for the victory (like prophesying or claiming the victory).

The Greek word for spirits in the Bible is: Strong's # 4151. πνεῦμα pneuma pnyoo'-mah; a current of air, i.e. breath (blast) or a breeze;

Shouting is like "splitting" the air, or "splitting" the spirits. This in our physical world is like an army splitting the ranks of the enemy army, like a "piercing" rapid and forceful advance through the enemy's front lines arrayed against us. We call this a "**BREAKTHROUGH**".

Other ways of splitting the air are by making other loud, sharp, noises with your other tools of personal spiritual warfare. Those other ways of splitting the air include, but are not limited to: trumpets, clapping, pounding on something (making a sound like a drum), etc.

## L.  Claim Territory/Seal off your TURF
God wants us to take control, keep control, and keep the enemy out. This goes along with the beginning of this book, where it was stated that God wanted us to have dominion over every living thing in this world. **We are claiming our territory or "TURF", and sealing it off from invasion by the enemy.**

*Joshua 1:3 Every place that the sole of your foot shall tread upon, that have I given unto you, as I said unto Moses.*
*Joshua 1:4 From the wilderness and this Lebanon even unto the great river, the river Euphrates, all the land of the Hittites, and unto the great sea toward the going down of the sun, shall be your coast.*
*Joshua 1:5 There shall not any man be able to stand before thee all the days of thy life: as I was with Moses, {so} I will be with thee: I will not fail thee, nor forsake thee.*

But the devil wants control.

*John 10:10 The thief cometh not, but for to [steal], and to kill, and to destroy: I am come that they might have life, and that they might have {it} more abundantly.*

As an example, it was stated earlier that the blood of Jesus is powerful. There is power in the blood of Jesus to destroy the works of the devil. Therefore, you can loudly speak something like:

**"In the name of Jesus Christ, I plead the blood of Jesus <u>over, under, around and through</u> my home, my family, and all that we are steward over. I declare this to be a sanctuary of God. I command demons not to come into this sanctuary, and I command all demons that are already in this sanctuary to get**

## out NOW!  In Jesus name!"

This is like creating a 3-dimensional protective barrier, or bubble around our **TURF**, and cleaning it out in the process.  We do this every day, at least once.  It takes about 10 seconds, but prevents so many problems.  Remember, an army, including us, always wants the battle to be in the enemy's territory rather than having the enemy fighting in our own territory, damaging and destroying things and people in our territory/TURF.  There will always be damage in the area of a battle.  Where do you want the damage to be, in the battles in your life?

Thomas Velez

## CHAPTER 7  Physical Actions


## A.  Dancing

Dancing has been used in the Bible to do spiritual warfare.  It is a way of praising God with our bodies.  It demonstrates our attitude and commitment to God.  In doing so, God fights on our behalf, much more effectively than we could.

> *Psalms 149:1 Praise ye the LORD. Sing unto the LORD a new song, {and} his praise in the congregation of saints.*
> *Psalms 149:2 Let Israel rejoice in him that made him: let the children of Zion be joyful in their King.*
> *Psalms 149:3 Let them **praise his name in the dance**: let them sing praises unto him with the timbrel and harp.*
> *Psalms 149:4 For the LORD taketh pleasure in his people: he will beautify the meek with salvation.*
> *Psalms 149:5 Let the saints be joyful in glory: let them sing aloud upon their beds.*
> *Psalms 149:6 **{Let} the high {praises} of God {be} in their mouth, and a twoedged sword in their hand**;*
> *Psalms 149:7 **To execute vengeance upon the heathen, {and} punishments upon the people;***
> *Psalms 149:8 **To bind their kings with chains, and their nobles with fetters of iron;***

*Psalms 149:9* **To execute upon them the judgment written: this honour have all his saints.** *Praise ye the LORD.*

We as saints, on our own, could not bind kings and nobles and execute judgment upon them, because they rule the natural world. But, they do not rule the spiritual world, and they are not more powerful than God. When God fights on our side, they are in trouble, not us. So praising God in the dance is an effective and even powerful weapon of God given to us for spiritual warfare.

> *Exodus 15:19 For the horse of Pharaoh went in with his chariots and with his horsemen into the sea, and the LORD brought again the waters of the sea upon them;*
> *but the children of Israel went on dry {land} in the midst of the sea.*
> *Exodus 15:20 And Miriam the prophetess, the sister of Aaron, took a timbrel in her hand; and all the women went out after her with timbrels and with dances.*
> *Exodus 15:21 And Miriam answered them, Sing ye to the LORD, for he hath triumphed gloriously; the horse and his rider hath he thrown into the sea.*

**B. Stomping or crushing with your feet:**
Like dancing, stomping our feet with the recognition and intent that we are stomping on the enemy is an effective way to move from the natural world to the spiritual world in our

spiritual warfare for the things of God.  We can also do this while dancing, if we do it with the intent of spiritual warfare.

Against Israel:
> *Ezekiel 6:11 Thus saith the Lord GOD; Smite with thine hand, and **stamp** with thy foot, and say, Alas for all the evil abominations of the house of Israel! for*
> *they shall fall by the sword, by the famine, and by the pestilence.*
> *Ezekiel 6:12 He that is far off shall die of the pestilence; and he that is near shall*
> *fall by the sword; and he that remaineth and is besieged shall die by*
> *the famine: thus will I accomplish my fury upon them.*

About Moses destroying the golden calf and praying to God to spare Aaron:
> *Deuteronomy 9:20*
> *And the LORD was very angry with Aaron to have destroyed him: and I*
> *prayed for Aaron also the same time.*
> *Deuteronomy 9:21 And I took your sin, the calf which ye had made, and burnt it with fire, and **stamped** it, {and} ground {it} very small, {even} until it was as small as dust: and I cast the dust thereof into the brook that descended out of the mount.*

About King Josiah cleansing the Temple:
> *2 Kings 23:5 And he put down the*

*idolatrous priests, whom the kings of Judah had*
*ordained to burn incense in the high places in the cities of Judah, and in the places round about Jerusalem; them also that burned incense unto Baal, to the sun, and to the moon, and to the planets, and to all the host of heaven.*
*2 Kings 23:6 And he brought out the grove from the house of the LORD, without Jerusalem, unto the brook Kidron, and burned it at the brook Kidron, and* **stamped** *{it} small to powder, and cast the powder thereof upon the graves of the children of the people.*

*2 Kings 23:15*
*Moreover the altar that {was} at Bethel, {and} the high place which Jeroboam the son of Nebat, who made Israel to sin, had made, both that altar and the high place he brake down, and burned the high place, {and}* **stamped** *{it} small to powder, and burned the grove.*
*2 Kings 23:16 And as* **Josiah** *turned himself, he spied the sepulchres that {were} there in the mount, and sent, and took the bones out of the sepulchres, and burned {them} upon the altar, and polluted it, according to the word of the LORD which the man of God proclaimed, who proclaimed these words.*

About King Asa, destroying a pagan idol:

> *2 Chronicles 15:16 And also {concerning} Maachah the mother of Asa the king, he removed her from {being} queen, because she had made an idol in a grove: and Asa cut down her idol, and **[stamped]** {it}, and burnt {it} at the brook Kidron.*

About Elisha to King Jehoash against the Syrians:

> *2 Kings 13:14 Now Elisha was fallen sick of his sickness whereof he died. And Joash the king of Israel came down unto him, and wept over his face, and said, O my father, my father, the chariot of Israel, and the horsemen thereof."*
>
> *2 Kings 13:15 And Elisha said unto him, Take bow and arrows. And he took unto him bow and arrows.*
>
> *2 Kings 13:16 And he said to the king of Israel, Put thine hand upon the bow. And he put his hand {upon it}: and Elisha put his hands upon the king's hands.*
>
> *2 Kings 13:17 And he said, Open the window eastward. And he opened {it}. Then Elisha said, Shoot. And he shot. And he said, The arrow of the LORD'S deliverance, and the arrow of deliverance from Syria: for thou shalt smite the Syrians in Aphek, till thou have consumed {them}.*
>
> *2 Kings 13:18 And he said, Take the arrows. And he took {them}. And he said unto the king of Israel, **Smite upon the ground.** And he smote thrice, and stayed.*

*2 Kings 13:19 And the man of God was wroth with him, and said,* **Thou shouldest have smitten five or six times; then hadst thou smitten Syria till thou hadst consumed {it}: whereas now thou shalt smite Syria {but} thrice.**

*Luke 10:19 Behold, I give unto you power to [**tread** on serpents] and scorpions, and over all the power of the enemy: and nothing shall by any means hurt you.*

## C. Clapping Hands:

This is used in two primary ways. First, to praise God-this may be with singing or dancing. Second-clapping hands may be used by itself or with some other direct weapon against the devil.

In the second application, like stomping our feet, when we clap our hands with the recognition and intent that we are slapping the enemy, this is an effective way to move from the natural world to the spiritual world in our spiritual warfare for the things of God. In the Old Testament, it appeared that even the enemies of God demonstrated their intent and commitment by the stomping of feet and the clapping of hands.

*Ezekiel 25:6 For thus saith the Lord GOD; Because thou hast **clapped** {thine} hands, and stamped with the feet, and rejoiced in heart with all thy despite against the land of Israel;*

*Ezekiel 25:7 Behold, therefore I will stretch out mine hand upon thee, and will deliver thee for a spoil to the heathen; and I will cut thee off from the people, and I will cause thee to perish out of the countries: I will destroy thee; and thou shalt know that I {am} the LORD.*

*Psalms 47:1 To the chief Musician, A Psalm for the sons of Korah. O [**clap**] your hands, all ye people; shout unto God with the voice of triumph.*
*Psalms 47:2 For the LORD most high {is} terrible; {he is} a great King over all the earth.*
*Psalms 47:3 He shall subdue the people under us, and the nations under our feet.*

**D.  Swinging Fists, Make-believe swords, etc.**
Swinging and making fists, "slapping", or even swinging and slashing with "make-believe" swords, may be used by itself or with some other direct weapon against the devil.  These are like prophetic acts, symbolizing our fight against the spiritual enemies.

We have seen, in visions, that what we are doing is actually strengthening angels of God, in enabling them and helping them in the battle against our spiritual enemies.  When we do nothing, our angels do nothing.  When we engage in spiritual warfare, doing such as these things, like swinging and making fists, slapping the enemy, swinging and slashing the enemy with "make-believe" swords, that these angels are doing essentially the same thing, battling in the spirit realm for us.

Bishop Bill Hamon, founder of Christian International, has been teaching and demonstrating this for corporate spiritual warfare. We have seen miraculous turnarounds in the natural physical world, even against armed physical armies or groups of terrorists, and national drug cartels, and corrupt leaders of nations. We have seen these things happen within even a few days of doing the spiritual warfare, and being announced in, both national and international news. So, we know these things work.

So likewise, they can work for us individually for personal spiritual warfare also. We can use these very same techniques and expect results also. In our own home, we can do personal and family spiritual warfare against the enemy, by verbally coming against them in the name of Jesus Christ and by swinging our fists, and "make-believe" swords, by stamping our feet and slapping our hands against the demonic enemies, etc.

Certainly, it would be hard for one to argue that there is something to lose by trying or doing this, except perhaps losing one's self pride, if that were of concern. But, we learn and grow in Christ, by experimenting with things that are done, and have been done, which are written about in the Bible, and that are certainly not forbidden by the Bible.  Who knows, but such Godly experimentation might cause someone to learn something new.

### E.  Marching Around:
Marching is a military formation.  Marching is also a sign of commitment as well as discipline and unity and obedience.  This is what God is looking for: commitment, discipline, unity, and obedience among His people (as well as looking for a few other things also).  In a time of war, these things as well as preparation are critical.

> *Joshua 6:1 Now Jericho was straitly shut up because of the children of Israel: none went out, and none came in.*
> *Joshua 6:2 And the LORD said unto Joshua, See, I have given into thine hand Jericho, and the king thereof, {and} the mighty men of valour.*
> *Joshua 6:3 And ye shall **compass** the city, all {ye} men of war, {and} **go round about the city once.** Thus shalt thou do six days.*
> *Joshua 6:4 And seven priests shall bear before the ark seven trumpets of rams'horns: and the seventh day ye shall **compass the city seven times**, and the priests shall blow with the trumpets.*
> *Joshua 6:5 And it shall come to pass, that when they make a long {blast} with the ram's horn, {and} when ye hear the sound of the*

69

*trumpet, all the people shall shout with a great shout; and the wall of the city shall fall down flat, and the people shall ascend up every man straight before him.*

*Joel 2:7 They shall run like mighty men; they shall climb the wall like men of war; and they shall [march] every one on his ways, and they shall not break their ranks:*

*Habakkuk 3:12 Thou didst [march] through the land in indignation, thou didst thresh the heathen in anger.*

*Judges 5:4 LORD, when thou wentest out of Seir, when thou [marchedst] out of the field of Edom, the earth trembled, and the heavens dropped, the clouds also dropped water.*

## CHAPTER 8  Mental Actions

### A.  Standing Fast/Decision:

There comes a time, sometimes, when we just have to stand fast, and actively wait.  We are not allowed to confess/speak doubt or fear.  We are commanded, as shown before, to be bold and courageous.

> *Joshua 1:7 Only **be thou strong and very courageous**, that thou mayest observe to do according to all the law, which Moses my servant commanded thee: turn not from it {to} the right hand or {to} the left, that thou mayest prosper whithersoever thou goest.*

> *Matthew 26:39 And he went a little farther, and fell on his face, and prayed, saying, O my Father, if it be possible, let this cup pass from me: nevertheless not as I will, but **as thou {wilt}**.*

> *Ephesians 6:13 Wherefore take unto you the whole armour of God, that ye may be able to withstand in the evil day, and having done all, **to stand.***

### B.  Fasting:

Sometimes fasting is necessary.

*Matthew 17: 19 Then came the disciples to Jesus apart, and said, Why could not we cast him out?*
*Matthew 17:20 And Jesus said unto them, Because of your unbelief: for verily I say unto you, If ye have faith as a grain of mustard seed, ye shall say unto this mountain, Remove hence to yonder place; and it shall remove; and nothing shall be impossible unto you.*
*Matthew 17:21 Howbeit this kind goeth not out but by prayer **and fasting**.*

When we need to fast, we need to accomplish it properly. Guidelines are given in Isaiah chapter 58. This may be a fast of food and water, a fast of just food, or just some portion of food, or whatever God leads us to do-but when we fast, we should do it God's way.

*Isaiah 58:6 {Is} not this the fast that I have chosen? **to loose the bands of wickedness, to undo the heavy burdens, and to let the oppressed go free, and that ye break every yoke?***
*Isaiah 58:7 {Is it} not to deal thy bread to the hungry, and that thou bring the poor that are cast out to thy house? when thou seest the naked, that thou cover him; and that thou hide not thyself from thine own flesh?*

So we see, there are many physical actions that we can do along with the verbal actions against our spiritual enemies, even though they may be working through people against us. **In all cases, we need to use the name of Jesus Christ**, in our battles against the enemy, because all power comes through Jesus Christ to us.

Thomas Velez

## CHAPTER 9  Bondage of the Threefold Cord

## Why Some People are not Healed or Delivered

# The Threefold Cord

Demonic (Spirit)

Stronghold

Physiological Problem (Body)

Catastrophic Events/Trauma (Soul: Mind, Will, Emotions)

### By Thomas Velez

Copyright © 2014  By Thomas A Velez

Many people are suffering from seemingly impossible or hopeless situations, either in their bodies or their minds, or even by demonic oppression. The people that I am talking about, actually want to be set free, and are completely willing to cooperate with the person or persons ministering to them. Repeated prayers for healing, deliverance, and for freedom from emotional or demonic oppression seem to do no good, and they continue on in their suffering. As this progresses, hope dims, frustration sets in, and a state of acceptance eventually becomes the status quo. However, there is a reason many of these people, who are victims, may not be receiving and walking in the healing and freedom and peace that Father God wants them to have. It is always God's will to heal His children (those that are Christians and that are following Him: not rebelling against or fighting God). Sometimes Christians mad at God, or rebelling against Him or continually and willingly participating in sin, end up coming out from under God's protection. This is somewhat like walking out from under an umbrella in the rain. Again, God and Jesus are compassionate and want to heal us, but they normally stay within the established legalities. But all the legalities can be overruled by a person's **FAITH.** Much has been written about Faith, so I will not expound more on that here.

*Mat 8:2  And, behold, there came a leper and worshipped him, saying, Lord, **if thou wilt**, thou canst make me clean.*
*Mat 8:3  And Jesus put forth his hand, and touched him, saying, **I will; be thou clean**. And immediately his leprosy was cleansed.*

*Joh 10:10  The thief cometh not, but for to steal, and to kill, and to destroy: **I am come that they might have life, and that they might have it more abundantly**.*

*Eph 3:20  Now unto him that is able to do exceeding <u>abundantly</u> above all that we ask or think, **according to the power that worketh <u>IN US</u>,***

One reason for these seemingly impossible or hopeless situations is because of "generational curses".  We have discussed this earlier, in Chapter 5 on "Verbal Actions" under section H, "Casting Out Devil in the name of Jesus". Cutting off, or breaking the covenant with, those generational curses is a part of setting people free. The verbal actions or tools of Chapter 5 should be used and have expected results before coming to this point.  We now go on to examine why some willing Christians are still suffering from seemingly impossible or hopeless situations, either in their bodies or their minds, or even by demonic oppression

The Lord showed me the following chart, during a prayer session at Christian International with several people in attendance. During the course of that prayer meeting, the Lord explained the meaning of the chart and gave me a scripture to help understand and verify the chart. The following is that chart, which I call "The Threefold Cord". This threefold cord is how the demonic realm is able to establish and maintain a stronghold in someone's life and to resist the spiritual efforts of Christians (prayers for healings and deliverance) to free them. It other words, this is why some people cannot seem to get healed or delivered.

Demonic (Spirit)

Stronghold

Physiological
Problem
(Body)

Catastrophic
Events/Trauma
(Soul: Mind,
Will, Emotions)

The triangle shown represents 3 areas of a person's life that can be "hooked" by the spiritual enemy.

# Threefold Cord **Ensnarement**

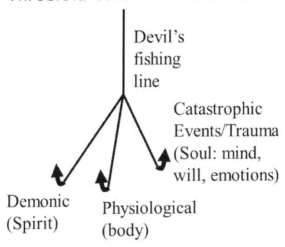

This is also like a fishing line or fishing lure made up of 3 leader lines, each having a hook on the end. Or you can look at it as being a simple "treble" hook (a composite hook having a hook on three sides). In this kind of hook or lure, to be truly free of the hook(s) or "ensnarement", the fish (or person) must be free of all three hooks at the same time. To be free of two will not be good enough to break free, and may allow the other two hooks to hook into the fish or person again over time.

All 3 hooks, or areas of a person's life must be dealt with simultaneously and overcome for that person to truly escape the clutches of that hook.

**PROBLEMS IN THE SOUL: Catastrophic events, or TRAUMA,** that occur in a person's life can dramatically and seriously affect them the rest of their lives. Serious trauma, hardships, accidents, attacks, rape, violent physical attack, childhood abuse, losses, etc. can affect how they think and react forever. It can generate feelings of hate, bitterness, rage, unforgiveness, jealously, inadequacy, low self-esteem, guilt, anxiety, fear, resentment, depression, despair, split-personalities, etc. and affect how they view other races, religions, gender, nations, animals, economic classes, education or certain vocations, etc. Counseling, both Christian and secular counseling attempts to deal with these issues to try to come to a healthy conclusion. Usually, in this arena, we are talking about attitudes and emotions that have developed as a result of these events. These can be both felt and chosen (emotional and rational).

**PROBLEMS IN THE BODY: Physiological problems** in a person's life would include problems of the human body, such as infirmities, sicknesses, diseases, degenerative conditions, chemical or hormonal imbalances, systemic problems (such as endocrine system, nervous system, circulatory system, respiratory system, digestive system, urinary track, immune system),

or other problems with the physical human body
and its proper functioning.  Doctors, nutritionists,
dentists, and numerous specialists attempt to
bring healing to the human body, and have much
success doing this.  Sometimes these physical
problems are self-inflicted, such as :

smoking, excessive drinking or drugs,

excessive eating-especially eating sugar,
and the person must repent and change their
lifestyle.

Also, ministers and other Christians, believing the
Bible, pray for people's healing, and also see
many people healed, both miraculously and over
time.  However, the ultimate object in all this is to
stop all degenerative processes, and for the body
to be restored to proper, pain free, functioning.
And, as we know, not all people are healed, either
by secular or Christian practioners.

**PROBLEMS IN THE SPIRIT:  Demonic
problems** would include repetitive or addictive
problems not in the physiological realm.  They
include amplifying, agitating and maintaining the
feelings generated by catastrophic events, and
lesser events, lusts and selfish desires, pride,
rebellion, and the numerous items mentioned in
the Bible.  Demons have personalities that can be
identified by the characteristic traits, or habits, or
influences on the victim's mind, will, emotions,
or sometimes even their body.  Yes, Christians
can have demonic problems.  We are all in this
world, and this world is full of demons, angels,

and problems of all kinds. Christians are not exempt, but we know the One who is greater than all others, and can set us free: Jesus Christ.

Each of the three corners of the triangle represents, like a hook into the victim  Each hook retains the victim in its' grasp. Each hook also helps the other hooks maintain their grasp on the victim. A particular catastrophic event might lead to a self destructive mindset, such as depression, which may lead to not eating or exercising properly, and may lead to a demonic depression with a lack of hope or even will to live or to commit suicide. Similarly, an extended sickness with pain may lead a person to quit trying to recover, and use excessive drugs to escape, and even listen to demonic temptations to commit suicide. As can be seen, the multiple hooks can strengthen each other grip on the person, and as we know, the demonic realm will try to use anything to its advantage, to steal, kill, and destroy.

We tend to try to help the victim by ministering to one of these hooks, such as praying for a sickness, etc. However, if just one of those hooks is released and the victim is set free of that influence/problem, it must be noticed that the other two hooks are still holding the victim captive. If much time goes by without the other two hooks also being released, then it is quite possible that the third hook (which was released) will be able to re-attach itself to the victim, since the victim was not able to move away from that stronghold.

**To really set a captive/victim free, all three hooks must be released,
from the body, soul, and spirit,
for the captive/person/victim to actually move away from and get free
from the stronghold that has been built up in their life.**

It is not the intent of this pamphlet to address how to deliver people from demonic problems, or how to counsel them, or how to heal them.   There have been many very good books addressing each of these topics.  There have been a great many leaders, teachers, and pioneers in these fields, within the Christian realm, such as Derek Prince, Oral Roberts, and Charles and Frances Hunter, Frank and Ida Mae Hammond, AB Simpson, Bob and Sharon Parkes to name just a few.  The intent of this pamphlet is to reveal or re-emphasize the need to minister to the needy victim, in all three areas of their captivity.

The following scripture emphasizes the strength of a threefold cord, no matter who or what is using it: for good or for evil..

*Ecc 4:12  And if one prevail against him, two shall withstand him; and a threefold cord is not quickly broken.*

Thomas Velez

## CHAPTER 10  Jesus Reigns

When all is said and done, God and Jesus shall reign forever.

*Luke 1:31  And, behold, thou shalt conceive in thy womb, and bring forth a son, and shalt call his name **JESUS.***
*32  **He shall be great, and shall be called the Son of the Highest:** and the Lord God shall give unto him the throne of his father David:*
*33  And **He shall reign over the house of Jacob for ever; and of His kingdom there shall be no end.***

*Re 11:15  And the seventh angel sounded; and there were great voices in heaven, saying, **The kingdoms of this world are become the kingdoms of our Lord, and of his Christ; and He shall reign for ever and ever.***

Thomas Velez

# CHAPTER 11  Salvation

## There is only one way to God and Heaven:

*1 Tim 2:5 For there is one God, and one mediator between God and men, the man Christ Jesus;*

*John 14:6  Jesus saith unto him, I am the way, the truth, and the life: no man cometh unto the Father, but by me.*

## All have sinned:

*Rom 3:10 As it is written, There is none righteous, no, not one:*

*Rom 3:23 For all have sinned, and come short of the glory of God;*

## The punishment for sins is spiritual "death" which is condemnation to the lake of fire/hell where the ungodly will suffer forever.

*Rom 6:23 For the wages of sin is death; but the gift of God is eternal life through Jesus Christ our Lord.*

*Mat 25:41 Then shall he say also unto them on the left hand, Depart from me, ye cursed, into everlasting fire, prepared for the devil and his angels:*

*Mat 25:42 For I was an hungred, and ye gave me no meat: I was thirsty, and ye gave me no drink:*
*Mat 25:43 I was a stranger, and ye took me not in: naked, and ye clothed me not: sick, and in prison, and ye visited me not.*
*Mat 25:44 Then shall they also answer him, saying, Lord, when saw we thee an hungred, or athirst, or a stranger, or naked, or sick, or in prison, and did not minister unto thee?*
*Mat 25:45 Then shall he answer them, saying, Verily I say unto you, Inasmuch as ye did it not to one of the least of these, ye did it not to me.*
*Mat 25:46 And these shall go away into everlasting punishment: but the righteous into life eternal.*

*Mark 9:43 And if thy hand offend thee, cut it off: it is better for thee to enter into life maimed, than having two hands to go into hell, into the fire that never shall be quenched:*
*Mark 9:44 Where their worm dieth not, and the fire is not quenched.*

**We need a savior, we cannot earn our salvation, but God loved us so much He made a way for us by sending Jesus, and Jesus died willingly for us:**

*John 3:16 For God so loved the world, that he gave his only begotten Son, that whosoever believeth in him should not perish, but have everlasting life.*

*John 3: 17 For God sent not his Son into the world to condemn the world; but that the world through him might be saved.*
*John 3:18 He that believeth on him is not condemned: but he that believeth not is condemned already, because he hath not believed in the name of the only begotten Son of God.*

*Eph 2:8 For by grace are ye saved through faith; and that not of yourselves: it is the gift of God:*
*Eph 2:9 Not of works, lest any man should boast.*

**Who can be saved:**
*Rom 10:13 For whosoever shall call upon the name of the Lord shall be saved.*

**How to get saved:**
*Rom 10:9 That if thou shalt confess with thy mouth the Lord Jesus, and shalt believe in thine heart that God hath raised him from the dead, thou shalt be saved.*
*Rom 10:10 For with the heart man believeth unto righteousness; and with the mouth confession is made unto salvation.*
**If you freely choose to be saved, believe and say something like this:**

> **Jesus, I believe you are the Son of God and died for my sins.  I believe that God raised you from the dead.  I ask you to forgive me of my past and come into my life forever.  Save me and help me.  I love you.  Amen.**

**If you believed and did that, you can be assured that you have eternal life.**

*1 John 5:12 He that hath the Son hath life; and he that hath not the Son of God hath not life.*
*1 John 5:13 These things have I written unto you that believe on the name of the Son of God; that ye may know that ye have eternal life, and that ye may believe on the name of the Son of God.*

**Then**:
1. Go tell someone that you accepted Jesus as your savior.
2. Begin to read the Bible every day if possible. A good place to begin is in John or Matthew.
3. Find a good Bible believing Church and that also believes in the gifts of the Spirit as described in 1 Corinthians chapter 12:7-11, including the gift of speaking in tongues, and attend it regularly.
4. After you have made the choice to receive Jesus as your savior, get baptized in water, by immersion into the water, like Jesus did.
5. Ask someone you trust that has the "Baptism of the Holy Ghost" and speaks in tongues, to lead you into that also. If you know of nobody that does, ask God directly to baptize you in the Holy Ghost with the evidence of speaking in tongues.

**Contact Information**

Thomas Velez
At:
**ThomasVelez.com**

Website: order more books by Thomas Velez
At:

**ThomasVelez.com**

Or at:

**Amazon.com**

Made in the USA
Columbia, SC
08 January 2020